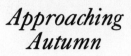

Approaching
Autumn

Also by Elise Maclay:

GREEN WINTER: *Celebrations of Old Age*

Approaching Autumn

Where Do I Grow from Here?

by Elise Maclay

Doubleday & Company, Inc., Garden City, New York,

Library of Congress Cataloging in Publication Data
Maclay, Elise.
Approaching autumn.

1. Middle age.   2. Retirement.   I. Title.
HQ799.95.M32   305.2'4

Library of Congress Catalog Card Number 79-6870
ISBN: 0-385-15553-0
Copyright © 1981 by Elise Maclay

FOR DAVID

"Joy, shipmate, joy."

Acknowledgments

The photographs that appear in *Approaching Autumn* were taken by the following people and may not be reproduced without permission:

Page number	Photo Credit
10	Garrett Browne Gibbs
24	Garrett Browne Gibbs
33	Tim Nighswander
43	Garrett Browne Gibbs
52	Garrett Browne Gibbs
71	Garrett Browne Gibbs
82	Copyright © 1980 by Georgiana Silk
93	© 1980 Ryon-Uibel Photographics. Photo by George D. Uibel
103	© 1980 Ryon-Uibel Photographics. Photo by George D. Uibel
110	Vacations and Community Services for the Blind, 117 West 70th Street, New York City
120	Garrett Browne Gibbs
132	Copyright © 1979 by Georgiana Silk

Contents

INDIAN SUMMER

Grand Tour	3
Unanswered Prayer	5
Second Marriage	7
Question	8
Brushwork	9
Social Security	11
Lunching Alone	12
Lines to Be Written in Liniment	13
Body	14
Free	16
Blessings	19
Bus Trip	21
Tourist	25
My Mother's Daughter	26
Job Offer	27
Cycle	29
Sauce for the Gander	34
Sage Advice	35
Florida	36
Grown Children	39

Mother's Day 41
Land 42
First House 44
Second Chance 48

FROST SMOKE

Country Road 51
Premonition 53
New Territory 55
Budgeting 56
Turbulence 58
Honorary Member 59
Worrying 61
Traveling Husband 62
The Trouble with Being Old 64
When My Husband Retires 65
At Christmas 67
My Daughter 69
Query 72
Transfer 73
Lawyer 75
Christmas Wish (Secret) 77
Grown Children 79
Patience 81
Lost at Sea 83
Helpless 84
Remarriage 86
Sioux 88
These Things Just Happen 89
Health 91
Miracle 92
Affluence 94

HARVEST

Old Sailor	99
To Be Honest	100
Spring	101
Lesson	104
New Career	105
Old Paint	107
Parental Guidance	109
Activity	111
Lesson Plans	112
Lost and Found	115
The Move	116
The Visit	118
Communiqué from Sunny View	121
On the Beach	124
Next-door Neighbors	126
Weather	129
Going Sailing	130
Free	131
Secret	133
Hotshot	134
Island Idyll	136
In the Woods	138

Approaching
Autumn

Indian Summer

...a happy or flourishing period
occurring toward the end
of something.

WEBSTER'S NEW
COLLEGIATE DICTIONARY

GRAND TOUR

I can't believe it,
Here we are,
Wandering around Europe like a couple of kids.
We always planned
To take the Grand Tour,
But inflation ate into our savings
And we more or less decided to settle
For backyard barbecues
And the *National Geographic*.
Then we started getting postcards
From the grandchildren:
Amsterdam, Copenhagen, Athens, Rome.
Fantastic. Wow. We may never come home!
"They go everywhere," Molly said, wistfully,
"Without a penny to their name."
Then she said (her eyes sparkling as they hadn't in
    years),
"Couldn't we do the same?
Fly charter, ride second-class trains,
Stay in pensions, guesthouses, rented rooms?
As for food, a roll and coffee will do for breakfast,
Fruit and cheese for lunch,
For dinner, too, if need be,
We've been eating too much lately, anyway,

And walking too little,
Oh Jeff," she said, her hand trembling on my arm,
"Could we? Could we?"
I couldn't refuse her, though You know
I was scared to death.
Of what?
Of discomfort, I'm ashamed to say,
Of not having things the way
I'm used to having them,
My breakfast egg,
Leg of lamb on Sunday,
The newspaper delivered.
Familiarity is comfortable,
It's also deadening.
I scarcely saw the flowers in our garden;
Today a meadow of poppies and cornflowers
Took my breath away.
Last week,
A snowy alpine peak
Satisfied me as no high-calorie
Meal ever did or could,
Though we missed dinner and the only food
We could find was a loaf of black bread
And a rind of cheese left from lunch.
But munching it at sunset in a field,
Our backs against a rock
Was peace and joy and poetry,
And my girl was there beside me,
Nibbling cheese, pushing back a lock of curly gray
    hair,
Her eyes shining.

UNANSWERED PRAYER

How satisfying it is
On this gray November day
To brew pot after pot of coffee
While I pursue
My own projects
At my own pace
In my own way.
Anyone I want or need to talk to
Is as near as the phone.
On the other hand,
Working alone
I get more done.
Have more ideas.
My time is not taken up with meetings,
Office politics, polite greetings.
Even the much touted
Support system
I had as an executive—
Secretary, file clerk, switchboard operator—
Got in the way of the
Free-wheeling creativity
That sparks my day
Now that I'm retired.

I never dreamed it would be
Like this.
Ideas tumbling one over the other.
I thought I'd sink in unstructured time.
Instead, I'm just beginning to see
What a lead weight the routine of an office can be.
Oh God, thank you
For not listening
When I begged you not to let them
Retire me.

SECOND MARRIAGE

Ours is a second marriage,
An astonishment.
 If not content, we had at least
Settled for closing doors,
And then one opened
And we walked through
To new life. Spring
Is the time for romance,
Yet now, approaching autumn,
We see every bough
A haze of bloom,
Every room
A blaze of candles.
Too world-weary to have imagined it,
Too tough to let surprise beget indecision.
In a calm with trumpets, we said:
I thee wed.

QUESTION

I met a friend I hadn't seen for years.
We visited and then he said,
"What are you going to do with your life?"
I thought I'd done it.
College,
Babies,
Cub Scouts, PTA,
A part-time job when the kids went away
To college.
I was so startled I found myself answering,
"It's a good thing you didn't ask
Me that question ten years ago.
I'd have said, go to law school."
"Why don't you?" he said.
"A woman I know started law school
At forty-two."
I'm fifty-three.
Do you think he knew?
It doesn't matter,
Because suddenly I'm excitedly
Thinking of things
I can do
And be.

BRUSHWORK

My friend and I decided to take some
Adult education courses.
You can't imagine how lukewarm I was about it.
I couldn't think of a single thing
That appealed to me.
Can't say why I chose oil painting,
But I did, and, well, you know the rest,
Painting's my life now,
I tremble with excitement just thinking
Of dipping a brush in pure color,
The canvas waiting like a marriage bed,
Red, blue, thunder, wonder,
I look at everything with new eyes—
For me there's not an old sight under the sun.
Retired? Oh, that. Sure.
But my real work
Has just begun.

SOCIAL SECURITY

Last week when I turned sixty-five,
Figuring, Thank God I'm alive,
I went down to the Social Security Office
To collect what they owe me.
They didn't see it that way:
"No check for you.
You have an income."
It doesn't "come in," I told them,
I go out and get it, earn it.
The sweet young thing behind the desk said,
"Here's a form,
Fill it out and bring it back when you quit work."
If I quit work
I'll be dead in a week.
"Young woman, are you telling me
If I quit work, you'll give me money,
If I don't, you won't?
Take your form back, sister," I said,
"You don't catch me
Signing my own death warrant."
Working's my life and I don't aim
To give it up easy. Of course, there's no way
At her age that she could understand
So I gave her the flower from my buttonhole
And said, "Have a good day."

LUNCHING ALONE

I had lunch today
(Leftover stew)
In my favorite chair
In a sunny corner of the living room
And enjoyed it more
Than any three-martini lunch I ever drank.
Probably because I spent the morning chopping
   wood
And was starved,
And with nobody there
I could lick the plate.

LINES TO BE WRITTEN IN LINIMENT

Yesterday I pried open a medicine cabinet drawer
That's been stuck shut for ages.
It was full of Ace bandages.
It occurred to me that I haven't needed one for
    years.
A message appears:
Nothing ventured, nothing sprained.
Well, that's no way to live.
Give me adventure, any time.
I thought I'd had my fill
But suddenly I'm starved
For the thrill of pitting myself
Against adversity, a task, a game,
The elements, a mountain, the sea.
We are too easily seduced by comfort.
But I'm not ready to amble off into the sunset.
I'd rather sprint.
Thanks, God, for giving me the hint.

BODY

I'm getting reacquainted with my body.
For years, I stuffed it into the
Proverbial gray flannel suit
And locked it in an office.
Hurried and harried,
I never tarried to marvel
At this miracle:
Plane of thigh,
Intricacy of ankle,
Eye opening, closing,
Like a flicker of silk.
Only when something went wrong
Did I notice and even then
Only anger
And when can I go to work again?
I didn't see
My waist thickening,
My face getting puffy,
We had become estranged,
My body and I.
Now I jog and play tennis and swim.
What a joy.
I don't look or feel like a boy

Again but I am thinner, tanner,
My stomach's flatter,
But what matters most
Is this thrilling sense
Of connection
With everything that moves
And breathes,
Sees light and shadow,
Hears the sound of wind,
Feels it on skin and hair.
How new it is
To be aware
Of being alive.

FREE

I hate to admit it,
But I'm glad the children aren't babies anymore.
I adored it when they were.
I honestly never felt tied down, I
Wanted them with me wherever I went.
They defined me. They meant
I had a purpose in life.
I was
A mother.
Other women had a child or two in tow,
It seemed, everywhere I looked,
Mothers and children.
I wanted to be part of that universe
And I was.
It was a sensual thing, too,
I loved the feel of chubby arms around my neck.
I needed
The clutch of their need.
We agreed before we married
That children were what marriage was about,
And it worked out.
We were a family.

We did things together,
As a family, picnics, Little League,
No dancing till dawn,
No trips to Capri,
But I never minded,
Never envied childless couples,
Was always glad to be
Me.
Amazingly I still am.
Glad to be a grandmother?
Yes. I confess
It hasn't much to do with
The grandchildren. They
Live pretty far away.
No, what I'm saying is that
It's unexpectedly delicious
To be free,
To go anywhere at the drop of a hat,
No calls to sitters,
To be able to stay away overnight,
Change my plans,
Dawdle, wander. I used to be
So rushed, in a library, in a bookstore,
Now I can linger.
I take binoculars whenever I go out in the car,
In case I pass a marsh or field good for
Bird-watching. I stop in and visit friends,
And go along with them if they invite me.
I park at scenic overlooks and look over.

Hardly anyone who lives here does.
I watch construction,
I see people staring at me with pity,
I imagine they say, That poor old woman
With nothing to do all day.
It's hard not to grin, because
I *feel* like Huckleberry Finn.

BLESSINGS

All around us,
Friends are retiring,
Like falling leaves.
It's unsettling. We've
Been planning to retire, too,
One of these days.
(Doesn't everyone
Living the American dream?)
But with no pension, we have to wait
Until we set a little aside.
But if we haven't by now,
How are we going to?
In June, Tom will be sixty-two,
And Christopher's not through
College yet. That's what we get
For having him so late in life,
Years after Alex and Sue.
But oh, what a thrill to hold him,
When I was old enough and wise enough
To treasure his infancy.
What fun we had with his boyhood,
And now,

How charged with excitement the air is
When he bursts through the door.
Some people have a retirement home in the
   Bahamas,
And some people, like us,
Have a Christopher.

BUS TRIP

Bus trips
Make me feel like a twelve-year-old
At camp.
Everything's scheduled.
Bags outside the door at seven,
Breakfast at eight.
Bus leaves at nine.
Don't be late.
Why should I be
With only myself to get ready?
Whenever Harry and I went anywhere,
We took the kids,
Even the baby.
Maybe we shouldn't have,
But sitters cost—if you could find one
You could trust.
Leaving the children for just a day
Made me nervous.
It's the strangest feeling going away
And not worrying now
About what's happening at home.
Nobody there—
Harry's gone and the children are

Married and on their own.
Lonely? I would be if I didn't keep busy.
Joining clubs, taking trips
Group tours, you know, so
You get to meet people.
A lot of the ladies are like me.
They never went anywhere without the whole
  family.
We laugh about how it was like
Moving an army,
Strollers and mittens and toys,
You can't travel light with kids.
I'd take two of everything so the boys
Wouldn't fight. At night
We had to eat early
Or they'd get tired and cross.
Once Jennifer lost the car keys.
Dropped them in a restaurant aquarium.
She was three. I can still see
The maitre d' fishing around for them,
Getting his rolled-up sleeve wet,
But captivated by Jennie.
(She's still a coquette.)
I carry her picture around with me,
Show it to the other ladies
When they show me
Pictures of their grandchildren,
As we congregate
In somebody's room
For a drink before dinner.

There are usually more ladies than men.
I remember when *that* mattered.
Now we're all just out for a good time
Like kids at camp.
Glad that we're free
Of responsibility.
Sometimes we
Sing on the bus—
Amapola, Yours Is My Heart Alone,
Row, Row, Row Your Boat,
My Country, 'Tis of Thee.
Nearer, my God, to Thee.
Nearer to Thee.

TOURIST

In Europe, I walked city streets,
Noting cornices and doors,
Arches and walls,
My eyes missed nothing,
Dogs, children, stores
Shuttered or open. I explored
Every lane and alley,
Paused at every square to look up
At the shape of sky the buildings carved out
    overhead.
I was on vacation and felt I could take the time.
Now that I'm retired I have all the time in the world.
Why not walk the streets of this familiar city
With tourist feet? See it with tourist eyes.
Why not rise before dawn as I did
    when I was traveling,
Watch the city wake?
Watch street life unfold like a flower?
Why not touch, taste, smell, be aware
Here at home?
Why not be a tourist in this old familiar town?
Why not be a tourist
In this old familiar life?

MY MOTHER'S DAUGHTER

My mother is eighty.
I'm fifty-three.
How can I be a daughter?
A daughter's supposed to be
A young slip of a girl,
Not a graying matron.
But my mother sees me
As a girl always. She
Holds a golden image of me
Secure behind her fading blue eyes.
I cannot grow old
As long as she
Is watching.

JOB OFFER

Be careful what you ask for;
You might get it.
For years I yearned for an exciting job.
Instead I took and kept a dull, secure one:
Wordsmith, Public Relations Director,
Finally, Vice President of a big company.
Dreaming at first of moving but never even
Sending out a résumé.
There were always pressing reasons
Not to rock the boat,
A wife, a new baby, a new house,
Kids to send to school, to college,
Then (suddenly, it seemed)
Retirement was staring me in the face.
The race was run. Now it was time
To sit in the sun. I made
My peace with the idea.
My life had been pleasant if not much fun.
Then, out of the blue, came this new
Job offer—as editor of the local newspaper.
They see me as "high powered,"
They say, "We'd be incredibly lucky if you were
    to consider it.

We realize we're sandlot and you're used to playing
   in the big league,
It might not be enough of a challenge for you."
Little do they know
The padded corridors of habit through which I
Come and go.
Have I any resourcefulness,
Any imagination,
Any creativity left?
My knees shake at the thought of the job
But I tremble with eagerness, too.
God, what a thrill
Running a show like that,
Being the center of the action,
Like riding a spirited horse
After plodding along on a nag.
There's just one snag:
Can I do it?
Obviously my old company sees *me* as an old nag
Ready for pasture.
Well, there's only one way to find out:
"Dear Sirs, I accept your offer."
Tally ho.

CYCLE

Together for thirty-five years,
We married for what we thought was love
But was probably passion.
We came to love each other,
Most, I think, when Jeremy, our oldest, was born.
Bill was an only child and the baby
Seemed a miracle to him.
He called me "my son's beautiful mother."
I was still young and beautiful then
And, of course, his saying so
Made me more so.
I'd wear lace
And tie a blue satin ribbon around my hair,
Present Jeremy, spotless, to Bill who
Every night
Would come home early to play with the baby.
Later we'd have dinner by candlelight.
But when Kimberly and Chris came along
All that flew out the window.
We bought a bigger house
Filled it with toys and noise.
I made friends, joined clubs,
Got "involved in the community"

As wives are supposed to.
Bill took a new job,
Began climbing the corporate ladder.
By the time the boys went away to college
Bill and I pretty much led
Separate lives.
I worried, but it
Seemed too late to do anything about it.
I should have prayed,
Gone to a marriage counselor,
Tried to get Bill to discuss it.
But I was afraid.
I didn't want to find out
That he had a girl somewhere
And was looking for
A way to tell me
That he wanted to be free.
I didn't want to hear
That he thought it would be better if we
Made the separation official.
In my mind's eye I could see
Him packing his things
And moving to an apartment.
Bad as things were with us
I didn't want that.
So he kept on coming home late,
Going straight to the den,
Burying himself in work until midnight
And then falling into bed.
I'd pretend to be asleep,

And keep out of his way in the morning, too,
Busy myself with chores,
Go outdoors and walk off my fears.
I'd talk to myself:
"After so many years,
Romantic love ends."
"Yes, but couldn't we be
Good friends?"
Then Bill retired,
They let him go.
It was a terrible blow.
I didn't know how to help.
But suddenly I felt him turning to me,
Wordlessly,
Like one of the children
Unchosen or left behind.
No sense saying "Never mind"—
You have to entice them
With some new activity.
So I coaxed Bill into helping me
Plant a vegetable garden.
"Only the heavy work," he said,
But when the bed was dug,
He wanted to know
What was to go in every row.
So we drew up a plan:
Tomatoes, leeks, parsley,
A work of art.
We hung it on the refrigerator door
To inspire us. We spent more

Time together in the hardware store
Buying tools and seeds.
I'm not saying things changed overnight,
But I have a feeling it's
Coming out all right.
We take walks together now, bicycle, swim,
Go to band concerts and ballgames.
In some ways
It's almost like our courting days.
Thanks, God, for helping us
Drift together
After drifting apart.

SAUCE FOR THE GANDER

At a tag sale, recently,
The most amazing collection of
Cooking utensils was on display,
Fish poachers, asparagus steamers,
Pots and pans,
And skillets of all sizes,
All well cared for and well
Seasoned with use.
"Whose are they?" I asked.
"Mine," said the woman who was running the sale.
"My goodness," I said,
"It doesn't look as if you would have anything left
To cook with."
"I don't. Last month my husband retired
After forty years. I've been cooking all those years.
I decided to retire, too."

SAGE ADVICE

My children
Are beginning
To tell me things
I've been telling them
All their lives.
Where were they when I was bringing them up?

FLORIDA

"That's it,"
Ken said,
"I've shoveled my last
Sidewalk.
We're going to live in Florida."
Silently, I shouted no, no, no.
At the same time, I knew I'd have to go.
Billy loved the idea,
"Hooray, we'll go swimming every day."
Gwen, sixteen, said,
"No way, Daddy, no way."
"All right," Ken told her,
"You can stay with Grandma
If you want to."
"I do," she said, and it was settled.
How clear and true
To themselves girls are today.
I wasn't raised that way,
But it was more than a matter of women's rights,
I saw how many nights Ken dragged in looking beat,
Too tired to eat, knew he was sick of running
After the carrot, knew the fun

Had gone out of his job, out of his life,
At the very moment his wife
Was beginning to get into things.
I was trying my wings
In volunteer work,
Considering getting a job,
Enjoying my new leisure,
Beginning to take pleasure
In the house again, now that the mess
Of babies was over.
I was in clover
And Ken in despair.
It wasn't fair.
I couldn't bear to sell the house.
Ken used the word "unload"
With relief in his voice.
There was grief in mine.
"I can't leave my family,
My friends, my roots,
I can't."
"Roots?" Billy said,
"Are you a plant?"
Well, what can I say?
I'd like to report that from the first day
I loved it down here,
But it wasn't that way.
I mourned the seasons,
I found a dozen reasons
To worry about Gwen,

And then,
Little by little, I began to see
That a wonderful gift was given to me:
My husband as he used to be,
Laughing and loving and open to me.
Whatever I left up north
Was small cost
For finding what I hadn't even
Noticed I'd lost.

GROWN CHILDREN

Help!
This is a four-ring circus.
Four grown children converging on me
In retirement.
I thought when I left the business world
I'd be done with decision making,
Problem solving.
Now it seems that's all I do.
The difference is, these problems are
Impossible.
Amy wants to know why I deem it inadvisable
For her to move to Aspen, Colorado, with her
    lover.
She wants me to tell her what's so great about
    marriage.
In twenty-five words or less?
Jess plays with a rock band.
His mother is afraid he'll get into drugs.
She thinks if we let him use the shed as a rehearsal
    studio
We can keep an eye on him.
Yes, but that will mean
Keeping an ear on him, too.

Jim's in law school. Whew,
One of them at least is all set.
And yet, his letters worry me.
He says he thinks the system stinks,
We ought to blow it up.
He's speaking figuratively.
I hope.
Jenny wants to open her own health-food store,
In the interim, she's working in one,
And trying to get me on a natural food diet,
Nuts and seeds,
Legumes and grain.
I refrain from calling it weeds,
Though that's what it tastes like.
No, the kids don't live with us,
But they don't live anywhere else either,
So they come and go.
They seem to arrive
More often than they depart.
How can that be?
We have enough bedrooms;
The problem is headroom.
Oh, yes, you asked about retirement.
Can I call you back
When things quiet down a little?

MOTHER'S DAY

I contracted with life
To have children,
Not young adults.
Lord, teach me some nice way to say,
"Okay, everybody out of the nest."

LAND

Land, once it's cleared,
Has to be tilled
Or it runs to weeds.
I'm a farmer,
I can't lie fallow.
Man needs
Reasons to live.
The seasons give me mine.
Spring planting,
Summer ripening,
Fall harvesting,
All part of a grand design.
The land,
Faithful forever,
Does its part.
As long as I have hand and heart,
I plan to do mine.

FIRST HOUSE

Being a minister,
Having a calling,
Meant going where You called,
Living in a series of parsonages
From coast to coast.
Pillar-to-posting it,
Mary called it.
But she went uncomplainingly
Although it had to be
Harder for her than it was for me.
After all, it wasn't *her* calling.
She didn't choose it.
She said she chose me.
But when we were courting
We didn't talk much about practicality.
We were in love
With each other
And with doing Your work.
We still are.
It was a good life.
But having a house of our own
Wasn't part of it.
I didn't miss it,

Never having known
What home-owning was like.
My father was a preacher, too.
We just about got used to one house
When we had to move to another.
My mother was careful, I think,
Not to let herself love any of the houses too much.
 Dutch door, bay window, rose arbor,
One house had a view of the harbor,
I kept a little rowboat there,
I cried when we had to leave,
Not the house but the boat,
I hadn't the remotest idea
What it would be like to have
A home of your own,
I just wanted to take my boat along.
Mary's childhood was different.
She grew up in a house her grandfather built.
A sea captain, he brought home
China from China, teak, ebony,
Prayer rugs, and a sandalwood chest.
The best room in the house was a
Room that he designed for himself.
Hung with maps and charts,
With a view of the sea,
Snug as a ship's cabin.
Mary said that she
Would sit on his knee
In that room when he
Was an old old man.

When he died,
Her father sat in the chair.
There was such comfort in that house,
She said,
The dead lived on in the things they'd made.
Hand-carved newel posts,
Braided rugs.
Her mother cultivated
Her grandmother's garden.
As a bride
Mary planted a garden.
We were called away
A year later.
She never saw her flowers bloom.
After that she pretty much
Settled for trying to make our rooms
Homey. Unpacking our treasures,
Hemming curtains,
Being careful not to offend
Parishioners, pretending
To be delighted at having
Everything done for her,
When she'd have preferred
Choosing her own wallpaper and paint.
Restraint is Mary's strong suit,
And a cheerful way
Of making the best of things.
I used to say
I hope God's making special wings
For her.

But You had something better planned:
A plot of land
And a house.
Ours.
I can see Mary from the window
Planting flowers,
Singing.
Imagine retirement bringing
Us this experience,
Usually reserved for newlyweds.
Imagine me
Taking a course in carpentry
So I can build bookcases
In our "library"—a former breezeway.
Imagine Mary and me bent
Starry-eyed over a catalogue
From J. C. Penney.
Oh God, how wondrous are Your ways,
Letting us end our days
In our first house.

SECOND CHANCE

Here I go again,
Nine to five
Alive and well,
Saved by the bell.
I thought retirement would be the living end,
Sold my business,
And went round the bend
With boredom.
Thought I'd never get another chance,
Then this company said, "Shall we dance?"
Turns out that they'd been looking for somebody
Exactly like me,
Offered me everything but the kitchen sink,
Had only one question, "Do you think
That after retirement you'll like
Working full time again?"
Will I ever?
Hallelujah! Amen.

Frost Smoke

---

*...an ice fog caused by extremely
cold air flowing over a body
of comparatively warm water.*

THE RANDOM HOUSE DICTIONARY
OF THE ENGLISH LANGUAGE

COUNTRY ROAD

I'm sorry, God,
But I don't think
Sixty-five is a swell age.
I'd rather be fourteen.
Yes, I have strong legs,
Sturdy shoes,
And a country road to walk.
I'm lucky
And grateful.
But I remember
How it felt to be
Fourteen,
Walking this same road barefoot.

PREMONITION

We missed connections last night.
He waited at one train station
And I waited at another.
I was calm at first,
Then panic mounted,
And insight.
I realized how much I counted on him
To give meaning to my life.
If he didn't come,
I didn't want to go home,
Didn't want to go anywhere,
Didn't care about anything.
I kept telling myself, it's nothing,
A traffic jam, his watch is wrong.
I had to wait quietly, composing my face
Because this was a public place,
But terror gripped my throat
And I couldn't catch my breath.
It will be like this, I thought,
At his death,
At his funeral. I cannot rant and tear my hair,
It must be a dignified affair,

Befitting his station. At his age
And mine, resignation is expected.
Who will understand that at sixty, seventy, eighty
It is possible to be
More in love than at twenty-three?

NEW TERRITORY

An Alaskan once said to me,
"The only way to deal with winter
Is to
Lean into it."
Leaning into it
May be the way to deal with retirement, too.
Holding back's no good.
Try holding back on skiis, and you fall.
All or nothing at all,
That's the ticket.
Everything in excess.
Yes. Embrace the inevitable
With derring-do.
But derring-do
Seems harder to come by
At seventy-two.

BUDGETING

Retirement income.
One day soon,
I'm going to have to figure out
Exactly what it will buy.
But I'm afraid.
Will we have to do without
Theatre, restaurants,
The cleaning lady?
I shouldn't mind giving these things up,
But I do.
Our children
(One lives in a commune, the other in a van)
Say man
Is too materialistic.
They scoff at me
For loving fine bed linens
Immaculately ironed.
They call me
"The princess of the pea."
I smile.
Intellectually, I agree.
Acquisitiveness is ugly,
Doing without has purity.

Yet when I visit them
I'm so uncomfortable.
Scratchy blankets,
Cold water for showers,
Granola under my denture.
Adventure
Defined as "roughing it"
Is for the young.
When we were young
We did a lot of what
I call orange-crate living.
Somehow it seems a bit unfair
That now when we've finally
Managed to get
A toehold on luxury
We have to give it up.
Yes, I can see
That there may be
A lesson in this.
But I confess,
It's not one
I'm all that eager to learn.

TURBULENCE

You calmed Galilee.
Calm me.
I am all turbulence these days.
I thought when I came to retirement
I'd have all my ducks in a row.
I'm an orderly sort,
But I don't even know
Where we're going to live.
If we stay here,
Can we afford to pay
The taxes and oil bills?
If we go away,
Where?
Can we bear to leave our friends,
Our garden?
Will we miss the changing seasons?
There are a dozen reasons
For selling the house and moving into an apartment,
And only one reason not to:
We don't want to.
I'm tempest-tossed.
You calmed the sea.
Help me remember Galilee.

HONORARY MEMBER

Today I was relegated to the ranks of women and
   children
And I didn't like it.
I learned how it feels to be kindly ignored,
Listened to condescendingly,
Patronized with flattery.
I attended a board meeting of my old firm.
They said, "We value your opinion,"
And made me an honorary member,
Denying me a vote.
They said, "It's great to see you looking so chipper.
Is that a new coat?"
A year ago, my haberdashery would not
   have been of note.
They'd have been too busy trying to get me
   on their side
Or trying to get on the right side of me,
Coveting my clout.
Now I'm out.
They hand me a lollipop and say, in effect,
Run along and play.
My granddaughter tells me women are treated that
   way

All their lives.

How awful.

God help me to stay mad enough to try to do
something

About that. I may be an honorary member of the
firm,

But I'm a voting member of the world.

WORRYING

Don't try to live your children's lives.
I've given that advice to others so often,
Yet I can't seem to take it myself.
My children are grown,
Have wives,
Lives
Of their own,
They don't need me to agonize over every decision,
Envisioning catastrophe.
Disappointment's hard enough to take
Without the necessity
Of breaking the news gently
To Mother.
I used to be so careful not to smother them
When they were younger.
Why can't I stand back now
As I did then and say,
"Why not? Go ahead. Give it a try."
Has the world become so much more dangerous?
Are they less competent?
Or is it simply that I
Am older,
My feet
 Colder?

TRAVELING HUSBAND

We're out of synch,
Leonard and I.
He's sick of traveling,
Says he's had it with jazzing off on business trips.
Now,
His idea of heaven is to putter around the house.
Are you ready for this?
He bakes bread.
The other night he said,
"Isn't it lovely having these quiet evenings at
    home?"
I said nothing, but I wanted to shout
"No."
Quiet evenings at home are all I've had
For thirty years while you
Dined in rooftop restaurants on an
Expense account. I know
He worked hard and traveling's not
As romantic as I imagine,
But all these years I've been waiting
For the children to grow up so I could
Spread my wings and go.
Anywhere. I'm starving for sights

And sounds, strange places,
The surprising faces of strangers
In airports.
And here's my husband
Whom I still adore
Saying that unless I'm looking for a lover
(You know that's not it at all)
I'll soon discover that
Travel's a bore.
Romance is in the eye of the beholder.
Maybe so.
I only know
I want to see for myself.
You understand.
You made Lake Como and the Vale of Kashmir
To dream on.

THE TROUBLE WITH BEING OLD

The trouble with being old is
Everything.

WHEN MY HUSBAND RETIRES

I hate to admit it but I've grown
Quite set in my ways.
My days are laid out neat as apple pie
And I have to admit, God, I like it that way.
How will it be when he's home all the time?
I shouldn't say this but You know
He takes up a lot of room in a room.
Of course, he can be a big help, too,
But where was he when the house was piled high
   with toys
And I got chicken pox along with the boys?
Where was he when Jennifer was teething
And Tim broke his hand
And I had to drive somebody somewhere every day?
I know. He had to go to the office,
Had to travel on business. He didn't choose to,
It was all he knew,
And he missed so much:
The clutch of baby fingers,
John learning to swim,
That sturdy little body, glistening in the sun,
Jenny practicing lines for the fifth grade play,
Music lessons, homework, jokes and games,

Spring, mud on the floor and birds on the wing,
And everything brighter and lighter
  because the children were around.
They're grown and gone now
And he missed it all,
Never really knew his children as children.
Sometimes he looks bewildered—
Where'd the time go?
Where are the children?
Why is it so quiet?
How will he fill the time and space now
In this strange place
Called home?
He looks a bit like Tim setting off for kindergarten
With a new bookbag and a trembly smile,
Hiding his fear.
Oh God,
Help me run to meet him
And make him feel welcome here.

AT CHRISTMAS

Forgive me, God,
But could you remind the world
That you were born
In austere simplicity?
Help me
Extricate myself from
Complicity.
In the hoopla that happens
Each December,
Help me remember
The miracle of love
That brought these children into the world
And brings their youth and beauty
Back to me
At Christmas.
I'm fearful and nervous and almost dread
The children coming home for Christmas.
It's heresy
To say that
And I wouldn't say it
To anyone but You.
I thought when they grew
Up and married and

Moved away
I'd be through
Stuffing turkeys at dawn,
Trimming a tree,
Feigning glee
At what I was too tired to see.
Every year
The children give me a housecoat,
Quilted or fluffy—
That's how they see me,
Comfortable and dumpy,
Which I am,
But I long to be
Lean and lithe,
Striving against a gale,
Climbing a peak,
Seeking a trail.
"But you wouldn't want
To be away at Christmas, Mom,"
They say.
Yes, I would.

MY DAUGHTER

I hate to face it, God,
But I'm envious
Of my daughter.
She's taking her junior year abroad,
In Vienna,
Studying languages and art,
Only most of the time,
She seems to be
Backpacking in the Dolomites,
Or skiing at Zermatt.
She'd be foolish not to take advantage
Of the opportunity
To see Europe while she's there.
I encourage her to.
I send her extra money
So she can take side trips.
I'd even be disappointed if she didn't.
It's just that I wish it could be me,
Not instead of her, but also,
And not as I am now, middle-aged and dumpy,
But as I was when I was her age.
My college years were so grim,
I was terrified if I got a C, I'd lose my scholarship.

It was the depression, and money was so tight.
I worked at night, and most of the time
I was too tired to enjoy anything.
And then, after all that struggle
To get my degree,
I never did anything with it.
I got married, and had three children,
The boys and Jessica
Who is everything I've always wanted to be.
She'll do wonderful things,
Have a wonderful life.
I'm so proud of her,
So happy for her.
And yet,
When I think of her, I ache,
With something which feels very like
Regret.

QUERY

Oh God, how I hate
The arthritis that deforms my knee
And cripples my wrist.
What an ironic twist
That I should be given immobility to bear
When I was revved up to battle dragons.
All my life I've made a fetish of being active.
Show me a challenge and I was there,
Hiking the toughest trail,
Playing every game to win,
Sailing into the teeth of every howling gale.
What does it avail me now?
How can I keep my vow
Never to retire,
To work till I drop?
REPLY REQUESTED AM DESPERATE STOP.

TRANSFER

Oh Lord, what do I do now?
When my husband died,
I sold the house
And moved, lock, stock,
Kit and kaboodle,
To this big, strange city
Where my daughter lived.
It wasn't easy at my age
To make new friends,
But I joined clubs,
Did all the things you're supposed to
Because I didn't want to get in my daughter's hair.
I just liked the feeling that she was there
Across town. Well, it's worked out fine.
She has her activities, and I have mine.
Now my son-in-law is being transferred again,
This time to a big city up north,
It's a promotion, more money, great opportunity.
Of course, they don't know how long they'll be there,
A year or so, probably, maybe less.
What a mess. I can't go
Gallivanting around the country with them, can I?

On the other hand, what am I doing here
In a city I moved to only two years ago?
I know my daughter's right—there are airplanes,
We can always visit. But what I want to know
Is where does this misplaced person *belong*?

LAWYER

I'm trying to hang in there
And not retire,
But I tire earlier in the day.
I used to work away all hours.
Jill would call at eight
And say, "Do you know what time it is?"
I didn't.
She'd want to know when
I'd be home.
Not late. Just a few
More things to get through.
She'd call again at ten.
Now I find myself
Nodding at meetings.
In the middle of the afternoon
Print blurs on the page.
Is it age
Or boredom?
When I was a young lawyer
Just being in a courtroom
Was exciting.
Now I know what everyone is going to say
Before they say it.

What's worse, I know they'll
Take forever to say it
Circumlocutionally, and then go over it
To drive it home.
My eyes roam the room,
I doodle,
Try to imagine my life undefined
By a lined
Yellow legal pad.
Does my presence add
Or detract from the firm?
Is my judgment valuable?
Does my experience amount to anything?
Do clients count on getting
My personal attention?
Or would they just as soon deal
With one of the younger guys?
I try retirement on for size
And am appalled to find
I've lost my identity.
A lawyer is somebody
Who practices law.

CHRISTMAS WISH (SECRET)

All I want for Christmas is myself
As I used to be:
Flat stomach,
Energy,
The ability to play all night
And work all day.
I don't mind the gray
In my hair—
Well, actually I do,
But not as much as I mind
The lackluster way I view
Everything.
Passion,
That's what I miss.
It's almost obscene
To kiss
Without it.
Yes, there's tenderness—
I don't value it less.
It's just that I remember
The flood of fire
That made everything

Worth everything.
Oh God, don't let me go to my grave
.Without one last
Sleigh-ride of desire.

GROWN CHILDREN

How agonizing to watch grown children make
   mistakes.
Jimmy has dropped out of law school.
He's so idealistic. He thinks
Somewhere—in business, medicine, the ministry—
There will be true
Justice, fairness, equity.
He'll spend his life and break his heart
Searching, being disillusioned.
Meg sympathizes. She lives in a commune
(she calls it a community)
Because, she says, the people there
Are supportive. Actually, they're supported
By other people—welfare, parents, me.
But Meg says I worry too much about money.
Money, she says, is the trouble with the world.
I agree, but I would like to ask her if she has found
An orthodontist who straightens teeth for free.
Well, I wouldn't want her to have crooked teeth,
But I don't want her to have a cramped life, either.
I'm glad to help out,
But I'm scared that I am merely
Delaying their confrontation with reality.

"Oh Dad," they say, "You and your old reality."
It was easier when they were little and fell and
skinned a knee.
A kiss and a Band-Aid could make that better.
But, oh, God, what do I do now?

PATIENCE

Sam's so patient with wood and metal
And so impatient with me.
Painstakingly, he'll sand and plane
To bring up the grain,
Again and again he'll turn a bolt and nut
Until the threads hold,
Yet he's quick to scold
Me when I don't catch his meaning
Quickly. He's cross when my
Conversation rambles while I
Try to remember names and places.
"Why can't you get to the point?"
He'll shout in apparent anger.
Yet I hear something else in his voice.
Is it fear?
Do facts and figures elude him, too?
Do I mirror things he
Does not want to be true
About himself?
He never was this way before.
I sympathize. And understand.
And yet sometimes I wish I were
Metal or wood
So I could
Feel his tenderness once more.

LOST AT SEA

One of my partners
Was lost at sea.
He was trying to sail a twenty-seven-foot sloop
From New York to Bermuda
In November. People said they couldn't remember
Him doing a crazy thing like that before.
Didn't he know at that time of the year
The weather's treacherous?
He knew. He was a crackerjack sailor.
I don't say he was trying to commit suicide.
I do know that he had watched his mother
Die a slow death from cancer in a hospital bed.
 I think he was fed up with playing things safe
All his life so he could retire in a year or two
And do what? Lawyering was all he knew.
And sailing. I think he decided
   to let the wind and the tide
Decide his fate
And taste adventure
Before it was too late.

HELPLESS

How can a man of seventy,
President of a corporation
Holder of half a dozen civic offices,
Husband, father, grandfather,
Admit that he
Is terrified of retirement?
At sixty-five I was sure I'd be
Ready to quit at the end
Of the five-year extension they gave me.
Truth to tell, of course,
When I said
In five years I'll go gracefully,
I thought I'd be dead by then,
But I didn't die,
And the years went by
Like the blink of an eye.
My desk calendar
Says the fateful day
Is a month away.
What if I refuse to go?
Chain myself to this chair?
Lock myself in the executive suite?
Picket? Refuse to eat?

I remember telling a man I fired:
"Nothing you can do or say will make
Any difference."
Today, for the first time, I
Know how he felt,
Know how it feels to be
Helpless.
It's like being pushed over
A precipice—
Or out of an airplane
And falling,
Falling free.
Help.
Help of the helpless,
Oh abide with me.

REMARRIAGE

Howard, one of Tim's business associates,
Made a killing in real estate, took early retirement,
And went jazzing around the world.
Now he's divorced his wife of thirty years
And has married—
I'm tempted to call her
"a young chick,"
But she's really a perfectly nice
Girl in her twenties.
We've had dinner with them twice.
Both times he arranged it.
Now he keeps asking Tim
What it is about the girl that I don't like.
To be honest, I guess I'd have to say,
What I don't like is the fact of her being his wife
And twenty-three.
At dinner she told me
She was about to roast her first chicken.
In the course of my married life,
I have probably, at conservative estimate,
Roasted one thousand chickens.
Chicken roasting doesn't,
As she would say,
Grab me.
But she's "into" domesticity,

As I gather she's
Been "into" T.M.,
Trekking in Nepal,
Experimenting with tea.
(Does that mean marijuana?
Don't ask me.
Youth isn't my native tongue,
Though with five children,
I have to try to understand the scene.
I mean, because they are *my* children and
I love them, I have to listen while they
Reinvent the wheel.)
I don't feel
The need for a twenty-three-year-old pal.
When the four of us are together and the men
Are making a fuss over her,
I feel old and sad. Tim says I'm jealous.
I am, but not just for myself—for Jill,
Howard's first wife. Her life sort of ended
    when he left.
His departure (I think of it as defection) came
    as a real surprise.
She was brave about it, generous and wise,
Wished them well,
And very privately went through hell.
She's still lonely and lost.
Oh, God, why should one person's happiness
Cost someone else so much?

SIOUX

At an exhibit
Of American Indian artifacts
I read words translated from the Sioux:
"If there is anything difficult,
If there is anything dangerous,
If there is anything courageous,
That I will do."
I wish I had made that my life motto.
It's not too late.

THESE THINGS JUST HAPPEN

I used to think
It will be better when Jim retires.
We'll have time to do things together—
Walk, ride bikes, canoe,
Go to the movies,
Take a college course or two,
Travel.
It will be good when
We have things to talk about again.
Silence has grown between us,
But slowly and surely we'll drift together,
Day by day,
The way we drifted apart.
My God, how could I know he'd walk in and say,
"I'm sorry, Martha, but I'm going away.
We've nothing in common anymore—
You know that—and, well, I've found a girl.
She's young and so alive
She makes me feel alive again, too.
You'll be better off.
And we just have to be together. We
Want to marry."
How could he talk in such clichés?

How can he live them?
And how can I
Bear it?
I can't say her name,
Can't picture them together.
That way lies rage,
At him, at her, at life, at myself.
What shall I think of then?
The children?
They're grown and gone.
They like their father's new wife,
They think their father's new life
Is cool.
How do they think of me?
As a fool?
"Oh, Mother, no," my daughter says,
"These things just happen, you know,
And it isn't the end of the world."
It is
To me.

HEALTH

What's this pain, this weakness,
This shortness of breath?
Death?
Time was when aches and pains were
Merely irritations.
Now they're intimations of mortality.
Is it just that before I retired I was too busy
To worry about my health?
Should I now?
The doctors say we should report symptoms,
Fight cancer with a check-up and a check.
On the Turnpike, Blue Cross has a sign:
HEALTH THYSELF.
So I guess I should go for a physical exam.
I used to like to—height, weight, heart, lungs,
A-OK, all systems go.
Now I'd just as soon not know
The state of my health
Or unhealth.
Of course, the important thing is not to be fearful,
But
I am.

MIRACLE

Last year
It looked as if I had cancer.
Fear paralyzed me.
I thought I was afraid of death.
What I really feared
Was suffering,
Pain and weakness long drawn out,
The need to be dependent on others.
I was more afraid of the process than of the result.
All the same, I'm glad to be alive.
No, let us speak plain:
I'm wildly overjoyed.
I rise each day with tears of wonder
In my eyes.
The miracle of miracles is simply to be
Alive.

AFFLUENCE

I used to worry that after retirement
We'd have less money.
We do.
But we have fewer needs and wants, too.
I don't need or want
The latest shade of eye shadow
Or custom made ski boots.
Flowers in a meadow please me as well
As a florist's bouquet.
In a way, lots of things we used to spend money on
Were substitutes:
A drink to ease tension
Instead of a walk out under the sky,
Restaurants and fast foods because there was not
    time to buy
Fresh vegetables and cook them lovingly.
A lot of things we used to buy
Were bought to help us make money
To buy more things:
Business suits, attaché cases,
Trade magazines.
Now we wear what we want—
Old, faded shirts and skirts,

Read what we want—
Beloved old books which
Have languished too long on our shelves.
We find ourselves avoiding shops,
Not because we might be tempted to buy
But because we hate to take time away from
Watching sunsets.

Harvest

---

*...a supply of anything
gathered at maturity
and stored.*

THE RANDOM HOUSE DICTIONARY
OF THE ENGLISH LANGUAGE

OLD SAILOR

Years ago I read a book,
Sailing Alone Around the World
By Captain Joshua Slocum,
Written in 1899.
Last year I hunted that book up,
Knowing that he, like me, had been beached by time.
Now, meaning no blasphemy, Lord,
That book is like a bible to me,
Telling me what an old sailor can still manage to be:
His own man, running free,
Self-reliant, adventurous
But sensibly taking precautions,
Routing foes, sharing his grub,
Measuring the sky,
Calm when storms gather,
Glad when they go by,
Eager for sunrise every day.
(A darling boat he sailed,
The *Spray*.)

TO BE HONEST

To be honest, God, I've used my job as a reason,
No,
As an excuse
For not doing things I knew I ought to do:
Visit my mother more often in the nursing home
Those last years before her death;
Go to meetings;
Write letters;
Collect money for this charity or that;
Pass the time of day
With people who seemed to have all day
To chitchat.
I'm a businessman after all, I'd say,
I can't be expected to have time to spend that way;
That's for retired people.
Now I am one.
What am I going to do
About my conscience?
Listen to it?
Listen to You?
That could be a bigger job than any I've had.

SPRING

It's Spring.
And here I am winging it.
No regular job.
No visible means of support,
Only an invisible one:
You.
I don't make too
Big a thing of that, God.
My friends would think I'd flipped my wig.
They make a big distinction
Between hippie kids
And an elderly gent like me.
I disagree.
Youth's the time to keep your nose to the
    grindstone,
Plug away, put something aside for a rainy day,
Provide for your wife, put your kids through school.
I did all that.
Now, cool rain on my face is important,
I can't be sure how long I'll be around to feel it
(My old office was air-conditioned and I never knew
What the weather outside was doing).
The kids are educated and Martha died.

Now, I'm ready for my big adventure,
The one thing I haven't tried.
Trusting You completely to provide
A bed, food, clothes, I need little beside.
In fact, having nothing anyone would want to steal
Is real
Freedom. And having whole days full of hours
To feel the sun and the green wind of Spring.
Autumn years?
My Spring has just begun.

LESSON

Since I've retired,
Things I worried might happen
Haven't.
They say you can't teach an
Old dog new tricks.
What about a dog who is sixty-five,
Glad to be alive,
And determined to learn
Serenity?
When You said, "Consider the lilies of the field,"
You must have been thinking of me.

NEW CAREER

I've been a physics teacher
All my life,
All my first life, that is.
I have a new life
Now, as the kids say, I am "into" botany.
By accident.
No, by Mary.
She worried about me
When I was forced to retire.
She knew that though
I tried to prepare myself,
It was a blow.
I was so low she had to coax me
To help her with her conservation doings,
But little by little, I got into it,
Prepared reports, appeared at hearings,
Did volunteer work at the nature museum.
Then the University asked me to do some
Research on rare plants.
Now I'm curator of a world-famous wildflower
   collection,
I'm writing a paper on a rare wild lily,
We go on field trips, lecture tours.

We're so busy, Mary and I,
But we're busy together.
Neither one of us is waiting for the other to
Get home, to get done.
That makes it fun.
We have a tiny apartment in town
Near the University.
What a change from our big old farmhouse,
But we love it. We see
Foreign films, stroll out of a Sunday
For croissants, have tea with visiting scientists.
Mary says it's like playing house—
A few cups and saucers and our books.
"Looks as if you've found your true profession,"
My son says.
"No," I say, only as Browning put it,
"The last of life for which the first was made."

OLD PAINT

The other night at a party,
Someone asked me what I did,
I said, "I'm an illustrator,
Or rather, I was."
"Oh, you're retired."
It wasn't a question so I didn't have to answer,
But I've been thinking about it.
How can I be retired when every day
I get up and do what I've always done:
Draw what I've read,
What I see in my head,
Cowboys and Indians mostly,
Canyons, cavalry,
"Shoot-'em-up bang-bangs," I call them.
You know, thundering hoofbeats,
Prairie maidens in distress.
Yes, I'm still drawing strong,
But the magazines I used to illustrate
Bit the dust,
Liberty, Colliers, The Saturday Evening Post.
Most men get kicked out at sixty or sixty-five
By some big company or other.

Brother, I'd hate that.
In my case, it was more a case
Of having one horse after another
Shot out from under me,
Making me a survivor,
Not a retiree.

PARENTAL GUIDANCE

When I was young
And didn't know what to do with my life,
I had faith that You had plans for me,
Had meaningful work for me to do.
And it turned out to be true.
Now when my son is trying to find his way,
I try to lead and guide.
No, let's be honest: I dictate,
Pontificate, and shove.
In love, of course. But he's grown,
He has his own
Ideas of what he wants to do.
Who do I think I am, You?
Help him find his place in Your design.
And grant me grace to stay in mine.

ACTIVITY

To be doing something,
Anything,
That's the important thing.
Years of being overworked
Have oversold me on the idea
That the ultimate luxury
Is free time.
I'm forever carefully carving out time
To do nothing
And finding it's not that much fun.
On the other hand,
Anticipation of activity is apt to be
Full of foreboding:
Walk? It's icy, I might fall.
Call a friend? They may be away.
Visit a museum? There may be no place to park.
Take photos? It's getting dark.
So many a lark, so many an adventure
Began with me expecting to be disappointed,
But going and doing anyway.
Remind me of that. Maybe I need to hang a sign
(DANGER. BEWARE.)
On my easy chair.

LESSON PLANS

I used to have to steal time
To read and write poetry.
Ironic, because I was an English teacher
And meant to make literature my life.
But teaching took so much time—
The classroom work, lesson plans,
Counseling, the bureaucracy
Of the school system. Some weeks
I seemed to have a meeting every night.
When I got home, I'd try to read—
Keats, Shelley—but it was a fight
To keep my eyes open.
Well, I'd say, some day, some day.
I didn't really think in terms of retirement,
And then suddenly it was upon me,
A cake, three-tiered like a wedding cake,
Speeches, hugs,
The Lake Poets leatherbound.
I didn't know they valued me so.
It was a lovely moment,
But when I walked down the front steps
Of the school that day,
I was terrified. What would I do

With all that time
Stretching ahead?
Teaching was all I knew.
True, I'd always longed for time to read and write,
But whole days? Weeks? Years?
Would I be
Like some zoo animal,
Set free and helplessly
Pleading to get back into its cage?
I took myself in hand then.
"What's eating you, Katherine", I said,
"Unstructured time? Structure it.
Plan your day the way you used to
Make a lesson plan for every day
Of every semester of English I and
English II. You
Have letters to write, closets to clean,
Friends you've been meaning to visit,
Enough money to take one European trip a year
If you stay in 'bed-and-breakfasts'
Which is fun but takes research,
Poring over maps. No time for naps."
I took to serving high tea
To friends who liked poetry.
I couldn't afford too many dinner parties,
But my friends had families to visit anyway.
They said my high tea
Was the high point of the day.
I guess you'd say

I took retirement a step at a time.
No lofty philosophy,
No grandiose scheme,
Just lesson plans
For a student of Life:
Me.

LOST AND FOUND

I'm sick of Esselen,
Of est,
And the rest of the
Navel-contemplating
Non-disciplines the kids are into.
I want to know
What they're going to do
With the selves they're looking for
When they find them.
In fact, if they were to ask me
(which of course they won't),
I'd have to say, looking back from the vantage point
    of retirement,
That the best times of my life
Were when I lost myself
In work,
Or love,
Some project great or small
That took my all.

THE MOVE

When I moved from my big house
To this little cottage on the country club grounds
My friends surrounded me with sympathy.
They said, "What a wrench it must be
For you to leave that lovely place.
You put so much of yourself into it.
Your cutting gardens,
The fireplace tiles
You designed and painted by hand.
What grand parties you used to have there,
Dancing till dawn
On that incredible lawn.
You must be heartbroken."
Strange, I expected to be,
But curiously, I'm not.
What happened is that the heart of that house
Stopped beating long before now,
When Ben died and the children went away.
A way of life that had been was no more,
And the house, with no reason for being,
Became a chore,
A frightening responsibility,
A senseless weight.

Now there's a new young family in the house.
They love it,
And I'm free,
Here in this cottage,
With a lilac at the door.
I tell my friends
I couldn't ask for more.
They don't understand.
They pat my hand
And admire me
For being brave.

THE VISIT

Traveling halfway across the world
To visit my son
And his new wife
Is like a fairy tale.
I am Goldilocks,
Trying beds, trying chairs,
"How charming,
How pretty,"
I exclaim, meaning it.
She says, "I sewed the draperies."
My son says, "She sews beautifully."
They tell me they found a desk in a junk shop
And refinished it.
All is neat as the proverbial pin.
Have they house-cleaned especially for me?
Has she reformed the boy
Who undid my best efforts
Ten minutes after he opened the door?
Who strewed the floor with his clothes
And ornamented the windowsills with cans?
We dine. There are flowers on the table.
She has everything ready, vegetables scrubbed,
Chops breaded, strawberries hulled.

All that is expected of me is to
Approve and enjoy.
Unexpectedly my eyes fill with tears.
Years ago I stopped hoping for this,
Frightened by what was going on around me—
Kids dropping out of school,
Friends losing children to drugs, communes, and
  cults.
Why should my son be an exception?
I'd raised him permissively
Compared to the way my parents raised me.
My mother didn't approve, but she said,
"He'll be all right, I'm praying hard for him."
Oh Mother, if you could see
How right you turned out to be.
He asks about you,
He says, "We must take lots of photos.
Grandma likes photos, you know."
I go to bed in a tiny guest room
Under the eaves.
In the master bedroom, their voices rustle like
  leaves.
My son calls, "Mom, I'll leave a light in the hall for
  you.
Is there anything else you need?"
"No," I tell him, tell You, Lord,
I have it all.

COMMUNIQUÉ FROM SUNNY VIEW

St. Petersburg.
A home for the elderly,
Euphemistically called
Golden Agers,
Senior Citizens,
Me.
I can't believe I'm here.
My friends can't either.
Actually, they're horrified,
Though they send me postcards
About the sleet and snow and about
How "nice" it must be
To be down among the sheltering palms.
The joke of it all is that it *is* nice.
Incredibly, I love it here,
Although I came more or less against my will.
At the time, I seemed to be
Giving up everything I'd struggled for.
You see, I came, as a girl, from a tiny town
In Iowa
To the big city, New York,
Dreaming of an interesting job,
Museums, theatres, an apartment

With a paisley shawl over the piano,
Exotic (to me) food brought in from delicatessens
Which stayed open all night,
Bunches of flowers bought at
Subway stands. All very romantic,
Yet amazingly it all came to pass,
Even the shawl over the second-hand baby grand
Piano in my apartment on Riverside Drive,
Rather a long subway ride
To my job on Wall Street, but I didn't mind
Because although officially I was a secretary
To a lawyer, in time, I came to be
What's now called a paralegal.
They entrusted me with tasks young lawyers often
   do.
I was proud, and it was interesting, too.
And yet, as year after year after year went by,
Monotony set in, and weariness.
I missed the sky. Cold made my bones ache.
Friend after friend married and went away.
My hair, my skin, my life went gray.
Then I got sick and came down here to recuperate,
Planned to return, but somehow, that never
   happened.
My friends think, how sad.
I think, how lucky.
Flowers everywhere. Air
Soft as a lover's touch,
Birds to watch through my binoculars
As I walk on the beach.

Millionaires don't live better.
There's a dining room here
Or I can fix something—English biscuits and
    cheese—
In my room. I can do as I please.
No one to say, "Take a letter,"
Though letter writing's my hobby.
Every day I have the New York Times delivered.
I read it with scissors in hand.
Clip out articles to send to friends.
I do the crossword puzzle, too.
We didn't used to have a library here
At Sunny View (what a name—sounds silly,
but it's true: it is sunny and there is a view),
So I started one. Got thousands of books
Donated, catalogued them. That kept me busy.
Now, I'm involved in local politics.
You wouldn't believe what's going on—
Developers, polluters raping the land.
Well, there's a lot to do,
And a lot of us to do it
Here at Sunny View.
As I was saying, my friends feel sorry for me.
I don't have time to tell them how wrong they are.

ON THE BEACH

How wise we were to retire to the beach.
When the year reaches
October
The summer people
Are left only with memories
While we have these
Incredibly clear days,
Heat haze gone,
The lighthouse blindingly white
Against the cobalt sky,
Waves dazzling the eye
With sparkle
As if all the pinwheels and rockets
From the Fourth of July
Celebration
Were called back
From their watery grave.
Marsh grasses wave
In the new wind.
Honeysuckle and bindweed wind
Our feet as we pass,
And the roses, wild roses
Bloom recklessly everywhere,

their last abandoned fling.
Would you like to do the same—
Bloom recklessly?
Have one last abandoned fling
On your own,
Without me?
Men do.
I wouldn't blame you.
I am relieved
When you call my name,
And show me a kingfisher.
There is more gray
In your sand-color hair,
The blue of your eyes is paler.
I feel indefinably frailer.
You take my hand.
It grows dark earlier these days.
We walk by the sea.

NEXT-DOOR NEIGHBORS

I love our next-door neighbors.
They're about our age,
Retired and trying to make do
But still dreaming big dreams
And trying to make them come true.
Young people don't understand.
They say we bite off more than we can chew.
Of course we do—
When you get to be our age
Small, manageable projects are a bore
Because you've done them all before.
Fred and Margaret are not interested
In having another little
Flower garden or vegetable plot.
What they're trying to do is
Live off the land,
Grow things to can and freeze
And put in a root cellar
Jim is helping them dig.
Raise enough strawberries
To have a big festival under
Our oak trees.
Our land's too shady to grow

Vegetables.
But it runs down to the water
Where Jim's big project these days
Is building a boat
From scratch—no prefabs or kits for him.
People say, "Jim why don't you buy
A nice little Fiberglas skiff and be done
With it?"
But he doesn't want to be done with it—
Boats or life.
"Being his wife must keep you hopping."
Of course—what do you think I married him for?
He was always this way. Now he's more so.
Up at dawn, busy all day
Building a jetty,
Clearing away storm damage,
Hammering and
Hauling and playing just as hard.
Our neighbor Fred's like that, too.
Last week we flew kites
In a howling gale.
Mine lost its tail.
Margaret's won.
When we were done
We feasted on crab cakes—
Jim's specialty.
He goes crabbing every morning,
And keeps his recipe
Secret even from me.
We wore costumes.

I made macaroons.
Fred opened an ancient bottle of port.
How lucky we are to have
Their sort
Living nearby.
Margaret and I
Sigh and say,
"Boys will be boys
Even when they're seventy-three."
But I know she's as glad
As I am
Not to be
Married to some old stick-in-the-mud
Who sits around all day
Watching TV.
Thanks, God, for Jim and our
Next-door neighbors,
They've made my days as noisy and
Messy and exhilarating
As life is supposed to be.

WEATHER

There was a time when the only time
I noticed the weather
Was when I was on vacation.
The rest of the time, I checked the temperature,
Tuned in the forecast,
Decided which suit to wear and
Whether to carry an umbrella.
But that's a far cry from tasting the rain,
Feeling the wind like sandpaper or satin,
Being enveloped in dawn, blanketed by noon.
Today, I paused in the parking lot on the way
To the supermarket.
I couldn't even see a tree, and yet, I swear,
The air smelled green.
There must have been thousands and thousands of
    days,
Ripe as pears on a tree,
Sweet as well water,
That slipped by me untouched, untasted.
Well, that won't be, from here on in.
Nothing on my list of "things to do"
Is as important as
Experiencing the day.

GOING SAILING

One-thirty p.m.
On a Wednesday
And I'm going sailing.
I feel like a kid playing hooky.
I've been retired for more than a year now,
But I still feel as if I'm getting away with something.
Which, of course, I am.
A lot of guys my age
Are dead.

FREE

For years of my life,
The years of my life, the months, the weeks, the days
Were organized by somebody else.
The idea of organizing them myself,
Of having a yearful of days to spend as I please,
Is dizzying.
Good thing time isn't money,
I'd go on a spending spree
And wouldn't have a minute left
For tomorrow.

SECRET

I've been retired now for almost ten years
And I've never been happier.
Friends ask,
"What's the secret?"
No secret. Luck.
When I retired, I owned my own business.
I didn't sell it.
If I can help it,
I never will.
Every morning I get up and say,
"I think I'll go to work today."
Then I allow myself the luxury of saying "No,
Life's too short. There are too many things
I want to do first."
Then I go and do a few.

HOTSHOT

Sailboat racing.
I used to be a hotshot.
Beat the best boats every time.
Sailed up for silver
At every awards dinner.
Good sailors asked my advice,
Treated me like a winner.
Now they say,
"Tough luck, old man,
What went wrong?" and I reply,
"I don't know,
Just sailing dumb."
But I do know.
The race is to the swift
And to the young.
I don't see as well as I used to,
Misgauge distances and overstand,
Lose my grip on sheets and situations,
Get rattled at the start.
I'm losing heart,
Maybe I should fold my sails
And call it a day.

But when the spray catches the sun
As the boat begins to plane,
I feel like a boy again,
Ride, ride, ride,
Over the bounding main.
Ready about. Hard alee.
I'd rather end my sailing career
In last place
Than with a DNF.

ISLAND IDYLL

We came to this
Caribbean island to
Get out from under
An avalanche of
Household chores.
Storm windows,
Screen doors,
Mowing the lawn—
Such omnipresent responsibility.
"It's too much,"
John said.
"Before I'm dead
I want to spend
Whole days in a hammock
Contemplating the sky."
I pictured myself
Floating about in a floppy straw hat,
Bringing him cold beer.
Well, we had to have somewhere to live.
So that first year
Was spent building this house,
Getting furniture here,
Putting up shelves,
Painting, sewing,

Things like that.
No time for hammocks,
Cold beer and a straw hat.
The gardening began
With a machete.
John bought one to hack his way
To the pump shed.
The next day he saw a coconut sprouting,
Decided to plant it nearer the house.
Well, one thing led to another.
Now every day he's out at dawn,
Cultivating a lawn.
I'm training a bougainvillea vine
To climb
Over the door.
Before we came, I said,
"I'm not going to take a lot of pots and pans.
We'll eat out of cans."
But now, the idea of baking
A fresh pineapple upside-down cake
Appeals to me.
Here domesticity
Seems basic.
Not added on
To life, redundantly.
We're stronger and healthier, too.
Thank God.
Doing more
Than we've ever done
Feels like fun.

IN THE WOODS

When we retired, we bought twelve acres of
    woodland
And built a little cottage in the middle of it.
Hemlocks whisper over the roof,
And a stream holds the house
In the curve of its arm.
I gather watercress for salads from a deep pool.
William grows vegetables in a clearing he's made.
We even have a lawn of sorts,
Dappled shade,
Where William and I
Play croquet—no gentlemanly game;
He's a killer and I show no mercy;
Whoever loses has to weed.
At night we read.
We each have a deep, comfortable chair
And a reading light.
Beyond the screen, fireflies flicker.
At the edge of the forest I know
That deer stand, watching us with gentle eyes.
One dawn a doe and her fawn
Were nibbling the lettuce I put out for Oliver,
The comical rabbit who comes each day

For the handout I obligingly provide.
We have foxes and raccoons,
Ragged asters in the fall and crescent moons,
Quiet days and peaceful nights.
I'm grateful.
And yet sometimes the lights of Paris,
London, and New York prick my memory,
Stir up in me a terrible longing
To be in one of those magical cities at dusk,
At the brink of excitement.
Contentment eluded me always
When we lived in the city,
And if we went back, I'd be exhausted in a day.
But oh, the way the lights wink on,
The diamond bridges, crowds outside theatres,
The clink of glasses in a restaurant,
Perfumed ladies passing,
The mystery of cities at night!
That's what I miss in the September of my life,
Knowing I've known it and found it cruel.
An owl hoots.
Dougal, the collie, regards me gravely.
I touch his cool nose.
He wants to know when I am going to turn out the
    light.
William closes his book.
"Come, Love," he says, "let's call it a night."